deep fry

deep fry

from stylish snacks to
sizzling main meals and
decadent desserts

LORENZ BOOKS

This edition is published by Lorenz Books

Lorenz Books is an imprint of Anness Publishing Ltd
Hermes House, 88–89 Blackfriars Road, London SE1 8HA
tel. 020 7401 2077; fax 020 7633 9499
www.lorenzbooks.com; info@anness.com

© Anness Publishing Ltd 2003

This edition distributed in the UK by Aurum Press Ltd
tel. 020 7637 3225; fax 020 7580 2469

This edition distributed in the USA and Canada by National Book Network
tel. 301 459 3366; fax 301 459 1705
www.nbnbooks.com

This edition distributed in Australia by Pan Macmillan Australia
tel. 1300 135 113; fax 1300 135 103
customer.service@macmillan.com.au

This edition distributed in New Zealand by David Bateman Ltd
tel. (09) 415 7664; fax (09) 415 8892

A CIP catalogue record for this book is available from
the British Library.

PUBLISHER Joanna Lorenz
MANAGING EDITOR Linda Fraser
SENIOR EDITOR Susannah Blake
EDITORIAL READER Richard McGinlay
PHOTOGRAPHER Gareth Sambridge
HOME ECONOMIST Sunil Vijayakar
STYLIST Helen Trent
PRODUCTION CONTROLLER Joanna King

10 9 8 7 6 5 4 3 2 1

NOTES

Bracketed terms are intended for American readers.

For all recipes, quantities are given in both metric and imperial measures
and, where appropriate, measures are also given in standard cups and spoons.
Follow one set, but not a mixture, because they are not interchangeable.

Standard spoon and cup measures are level.
1 tsp = 5ml, 1 tbsp = 15ml, 1 cup = 250ml|8fl oz

Australian standard tablespoons are 20ml. Australian readers should use 3 tsp
in place of 1 tbsp for measuring small quantities of gelatine, flour, salt, etc.

Medium (US large) eggs are used unless otherwise stated.

Deep Fry has been written with the reader's safety in mind, and the advice,
information and instructions are intended to be clear and safe to follow.
However, cooking with hot fat and oil can be dangerous and there is a risk
of burns and fire if sufficient care is not taken. Neither the author nor
the publisher can accept any legal responsibility or liability for any errors
or omissions made, or for accidents in the kitchen.

CONTENTS

perfectly fried

Hot, crisp and golden – these are the words that come to mind when you think about deep-fried food. Deep-frying is the way to produce the light-as-air batter that encases tempura vegetables, the crackle and snap of the pastry surrounding hot spring rolls and spicy samosas, the heavenly delight of the humble but perfectly golden French fry, and the sinful taste of warm and comforting sugared donuts.

Deep-fried food is enjoyed throughout the world, from the food markets of China to the chic and trendy restaurants in the West and from the bazaars and street food stalls of India to the rustic kitchens of Italy and the Mediterranean region. This wonderful cooking technique plays an essential role in almost every cuisine around the globe.

In today's diet- and health-conscious world, deep-frying is often frowned upon for being far too unhealthy. However, it is important to remember that most things, when done in moderation, are usually OK. As long as you maintain a balance in your life – take regular exercise and eat a healthy, varied diet – deep-fried food can still be enjoyed as an indulgent treat now and again.

CRISPY VEGETABLE SHAVINGS

FISH GOUJONS

DEEP-FRIED COURGETTES

This wonderful book takes you through the basics of deep-frying, explains how to make simple deep-fries such as crisps (US chips) and battered fish and vegetables, then offers four fabulous chapters of inspiring recipes.

PERFECT PARTY FOOD

The first chapter is devoted to bitesize deep-fries that are perfect for home entertaining. These delightful, tasty morsels are sure to impress your guests.

You'll discover a definite Italian flavour in the courgette (zucchini) fritters with garlic and mint, as well as in the tiny meatballs served with a sweet red wine salsa. Spicy onion and gram fritters, crispy tempura with ginger dipping sauce, and exotic coconut-rolled prawns (shrimp) with a spicy lime and peanut dip all draw on the flavours of the East.

AWESOME APPETIZERS

The appetizers chapter offers traditional deep-fry specialities including crunchy pork and prawn spring rolls, as well as Asian lamb and pea samosas with coconut and coriander (cilantro) relish, and a hip, bistro-style fusion salad of crispy rice noodles and asparagus. Potato röstis with smoked salmon are a sophisticated take on the Jewish latke, while crunchy risotto balls filled with mozzarella take their inspiration from Italy.

MOUTHWATERING MAIN MEALS

The wonderful array of main-meal recipes includes an updated version of a British classic: fish and chips served with a piquant, fusion tartare sauce. From the United States there is the simple but scrumptious version of Southern-fried chicken served with a crunchy Caesar-style salad. The Deep South meets Asia in crab cakes with coconut rice, and veal has never been treated better than when it has been coated in cheesy crumbs, then deep-fried and served with herb and garlic mash. A warm aubergine (eggplant) and fragrant herb salad with garlic ciabatta is perfect for vegetarians.

DONUTS AND DECADENT DESSERTS

In the final chapter there is a wonderful selection of sweet and fruity treats from American-style sugared donuts to lightly battered, deep-fried cherries, crisp wontons stuffed with banana and nuts and then drizzled with hot caramel chocolate sauce, and melt-in-the-mouth cinnamon and apple fritters. If you really want to impress your guests, try the ultra-modern crisp mango stacks with raspberry and passion fruit coulis.

equipment

There is an art to deep-frying and perfect results are dependent on a number of factors. These include using the right amount of oil, heating it to the right temperature and cooking the food for the right length of time. There are several basic utensils and pieces of equipment that are essential.

DEEP-FAT FRYERS

The safest utensil of all for deep-frying is an electric deep-fat fryer. Choose one that is very stable and has a deep oil container with a good capacity, as well as an efficient and easy-to-use thermostat control. Always read the manufacturer's instructions and follow them carefully to ensure that you use the fryer efficiently and safely.

LARGE ENAMELLED CAST-IRON PANS OR DUTCH OVENS

These heavy pans are perfect for deep-frying for several reasons. Their heavy base and thick sides absorb heat and hold it evenly, which helps to keep the oil at the right temperature. They are also very stable, which is particularly important when deep-frying.

When choosing a cast-iron pan or Dutch oven for deep-frying, make sure that it is at least 20cm/8in wide and 15cm|6in deep. The pan or Dutch oven should have a heavy base so that the oil heats evenly. It should be large enough so that, when half-filled with oil, the food can be completely immersed and is able to "swim" in the oil and not be overcrowded while it is cooking.

WOKS

These versatile cooking vessels make terrific deep-fat fryers due to their shape. They are wide and deep, which provides a perfect cooking area for deep-frying. Their tapered shape means that you need less oil to fill them than you would a classic straight-sided pan. The tapered shape also allows heat to travel up the sides of the pan, heating the oil quickly.

Traditional cast-iron woks are just as efficient as the modern non-stick models. Choose one that has a flat base as it will make better contact with the heat source, helping to maintain an even temperature. Ensure that you centre the wok over the hotplate or burner, and check that the wok is stable and secure before you start heating the oil.

DEEP-FAT FRYER

CAST-IRON PAN

TRADITIONAL WOK

SKIMMERS AND SLOTTED SPOONS

DEEP-FRYING THERMOMETER

WIRE RACKS

OTHER PANS

In general, these are only good for frying small, flat pieces of food. When using a pan for deep-frying, make sure it is at least 10cm | 4in deep and has a wide surface area. To be safe, the oil should be no more than 2.5–4cm | 1–1½in deep. Never fill the pan more than two-thirds full of oil.

THERMOMETERS

Temperature control is one of the most important requirements for successful deep-fat frying. Always check the recipe to find out the correct temperature for the oil before you start, as different types of food require different temperatures.

A deep-frying thermometer or a sugar (candy) thermometer is an invaluable piece of equipment. Place the thermometer in the pan while the oil is still cool,

then, once the oil has reached the desired temperature, remove the thermometer from the oil. (If the oil overheats, it can cause the thermometer to crack.)

If you do not have a thermometer, the temperature of the oil can be tested by adding a cube of day-old bread to it. If the bread browns in 45–60 seconds, the temperature will be about 180°C | 350°F. Another way to check the temperature is to insert the handle of a wooden spoon into the oil. If little bubbles surround the end of the handle, the temperature will be 180–190°C | 350–375°F.

WIRE MESH SKIMMERS AND SLOTTED SPOONS

These are available in all shapes and sizes and are used to lower food into hot oil, and lift it out. The holes in the metal allow the excess oil to drain away.

WIRE RACKS

Elevated wire racks lined with kitchen paper, or placed on top of crumpled kitchen paper, are useful for draining deep-fried foods. Fried food that is placed on a rack will stay crisper longer because steam, which can make the coating soggy, is allowed to escape.

TONGS

Long-handled tongs are useful for lifting larger items of food in and out of hot oil. Ensure that you hold metal-handled tongs with an oven glove.

OVENS

Keep deep-fried food hot and crisp in the oven. Preheat the oven to no higher than 110°C | 225°F | Gas ¼, then transfer drained food to a wire rack or baking sheet and place in the oven to keep warm.

deep-fry basics

Deep-fried food is usually protected by a coating such as batter or breadcrumbs, before being submerged in a pan of hot oil or fat. The sizzling hot oil surrounds the food and cooks it evenly, from all sides, creating an outer crust that seals the flavour inside. If the oil is at the correct temperature the food will cook perfectly on the inside and form a crisp, golden crust on the outside.

CHOOSING THE OIL OR FAT

The oil or fat used for deep-frying must have a high smoke point. This is the temperature to which the oil or fat can be heated without smoking. Fats such as butter and margarine that smoke at fairly low temperatures are therefore not good candidates for deep-frying.

White cooking fats, lard and most vegetable oils have a high smoke point and are perfect for deep-frying. When using vegetable oil, choose a good quality, well-blended variety with a neutral flavour. Any good brand name vegetable oil is suitable because all have been designed to remain stable within the usual deep-frying temperature range (150–190°C|300–375°F).

Sunflower oil, vegetable oil, corn oil, rapeseed (canola) oil, and groundnut (peanut) oil are all good candidates. Olive oil is stable at high frying temperatures, but it is strongly flavoured and will impart its own distinctive taste to the food. Never use seasoning oils such as basil, walnut or sesame oils because they will smoke at a low temperature.

USING DEEP-FRY OIL OR FAT

Oil or fat for deep-frying can be used two to three times. However, this is not recommended because each time the oil or fat is heated it breaks down a little more. This increases the oil or fat's saturation level and affects not only its flavour, but also its flash point – the temperature at which the fat or oil could ignite.

Do not deep-fry food at over 200°C|400°F as this will also cause the oil or fat to start breaking down into separate components, affecting both its flavour and its chances of catching fire.

Store oil in a dark, cool place. Never store it in the refrigerator because chilled oil will spit when heated. White fats and lard should be stored in the refrigerator.

CHOOSE THE RIGHT OIL

CHECK THE TEMPERATURE

LOWER FOOD GENTLY INTO HOT OIL

DO NOT OVERCROWD THE PAN

LIFT OUT WITH A SLOTTED SPOON

DRAIN ON KITCHEN PAPER

DISCARDING USED OIL OR FAT

To discard used oil, leave it to cool, then, using a funnel, pour into a large jar or bottle with a secure lid before disposal. Leave white fat to cool, then tip into a heatproof bowl and leave until completely solid, before discarding.

COOKING AT THE CORRECT TEMPERATURE

The temperature of the fat or oil is all-important. Oil at the right temperature will produce a deliciously crisp exterior and a succulent, flavourful interior. If the oil is too hot, the food will burn on the outside before it is fully cooked inside. If the oil is not hot enough, the food will absorb too much oil and become soggy.

The usual temperature for deep-frying is about 190°C|375°F. However, recipes differ according to the food being fried.

SUCCESSFUL DEEP-FRYING

1 Be prepared for a fire when deep-frying. Have a fire blanket on hand in the kitchen, or a large lid to quell the fire in the pot. (**Never** pour water on a deep-fat fire.)

2 Make sure that the deep-fat fryer, wok or pan is stable, then pour in the oil. (The food will absorb less oil if it can be completely immersed in the oil.) Ensure there is enough space in the fryer or pan for the level of oil to rise when the food is added.

3 Using a thermometer, heat the oil to the correct temperature, then carefully slide or lower the food into the hot oil. (This will prevent spitting.)

4 Once cooked, carefully lift the food out of the hot oil using a wire-mesh skimmer, slotted spoon or tongs.

5 Drain the food on a wire rack lined with absorbent kitchen paper. Alternatively, place the rack on top of crumpled kitchen paper and place the food on top of the rack.

TIPS FOR SUCCESS

- Avoid adding chilled food to hot oil as this will lower the oil temperature and cause spitting.
- Add small amounts of food at a time and never overcrowd the pan.
- If food is battered, allow excess batter to drip off before frying.
- Keep oil at the correct temperature.

coatings, batters and simple deep-fries

Foods that have a high starch content, such as potatoes, can be deep-fried without a coating or batter, but most other foods need protection from the hot oil. However, coatings and batters do not only protect delicate foods from the intense heat of really hot oil or fat, they also help prevent oil from penetrating the food, and they stop the flavour of the food from tainting the oil, so that it can be used again. Coating food in a thin layer of egg and seasoned flour or breadcrumbs, or dipping it in batter produces a crisp outer crust, while the food inside stays moist and succulent. Different types of food are better suited to different types of coating or batter. Thin small pieces of food that cook quickly can be simply coated with egg

and seasoned flour, while thicker pieces of food, and foods that require longer cooking, such as meat or poultry, need the heavier coating of a batter or egg and breadcrumbs. Some larger pieces of food may be coated twice to give them double the protection so that they can be cooked in the oil for a long time.

coatings

SEASONED FLOUR For the simplest of all coatings, dip the food in lightly beaten egg, then roll in seasoned plain (all-purpose) or wholemeal (whole-wheat) flour, turning the food until it is lightly coated all over. Dust away any excess flour and deep-fry in batches until crisp and golden.

BREADCRUMBS Dip the food in lightly beaten egg, then coat with dried, seasoned breadcrumbs and deep-fry. If you prepare the breadcrumbed food ahead of time, arrange on a plate and store uncovered in the refrigerator – the coating will dry out and, once fried, will be even crisper.

SUPER-CRISP COATING Dip the food in lightly beaten egg, then coat in a mixture of 100g|3¾oz plain (all-purpose) flour, 100g|3¾oz cornflour (cornstarch), 2.5ml|½ tsp baking powder and seasoning before deep-frying until golden.

OVEN FINISH Fry coated food until browned, then finish off in a preheated oven set at 200°C|400°F|Gas 6.

DIP THE FOOD IN BEATEN EGG

COAT IN FLOUR OR CRUMBS

THEN DEEP-FRY IN VEGETABLE OIL

MAKE A SIMPLE BATTER

LIBERALLY COAT THE FOOD

DEEP-FRY UNTIL CRISP AND GOLDEN

batters

A batter is a fairly thick mixture made usually with flour, eggs and liquid. The liquid may be water, which makes a very light batter, or milk, which produces a slightly silky texture and also encourages the batter to brown more quickly; beer is sometimes used for savoury batters because it not only adds flavour, but also adds air. Some batters have raising agents such as baking powder added to make them light, while others include yeast. Foods such as courgettes (zucchini), mushrooms and prawns (shrimp) are well suited to a batter coating, which protects them from the intense heat of the oil. Use a heavier yeast or beer batter for foods that are cooked for a relatively long time. For fragile foods, or those that are pre-cooked, the batter should be thinner.

BASIC BATTER This batter is ideal for quickly cooked foods such as onion rings. In a bowl, sift 115g|4oz|1 cup plain (all-purpose) flour, 5ml|1 tsp salt and 5ml|1 tsp baking powder. Beat together 1 egg and 250ml|8fl oz milk and whisk half into the flour mixture until smooth. Gradually whisk in the remaining milk mixture. Dip the food in the batter and deep-fry until golden. Drain on kitchen paper.

CRUNCHY CORNMEAL BATTER Whisk together 115g|4oz|1 cup plain (all-purpose) flour, 115g|4oz|1 cup polenta or fine cornmeal, 15ml|1 tbsp baking powder, a pinch of salt, 5ml|1 tsp cayenne pepper or paprika, 150ml| 1/4 pint|2/3 cup milk, 2 beaten eggs and 50ml|2fl oz|1/4 cup vegetable oil. Dip the food in the batter, allow the excess to drain off, then deep-fry until golden.

LIGHT BATTER Perfect for prawns (shrimp) or long, thin goujons of fish or chicken. Combine 25g|1oz|1/4 cup cornflour (cornstarch) and a pinch of salt. In a separate bowl beat 3 egg whites with 20ml|4 tsp iced water until softly peaking. Dip the food first in the cornflour mixture, then in the egg white mixture to coat it completely and deep-fry in batches until golden.

ASIAN-STYLE BATTER This is good with vegetables, such as thinly sliced onion or tiny cauliflower florets. Combine sifted 175g|6oz chickpea (gram) flour with a pinch each of baking powder, ground cumin, ground coriander and curry powder. Stir in enough cold water to form a thick but pourable batter. Season well, then dip the food in the batter, allow the excess to drain off and deep-fry until crisp.

simple deep-fries

Although most deep-fried foods need to be protected from the intense heat of the oil by a layer of batter or coating, starchy foods such as root vegetables, doughs, bread and tortillas can be deep-fried without this protective layer. Vegetables such as potatoes and plantain can be cut into wedges or thick slices and fried as they are. This produces delicious chips (French fries) that are crisp and golden on the outside and moist and succulent on the inside. They are great simply tossed in salt or spices or served with a dip or spicy salsa.

Thinly sliced root vegetables, such as beetroot (beet) or parsnips, or wedges of Mexican corn or wheat tortillas, can be deep-fried to make wonderfully crunchy crisps (US chips).

Because they are very starchy, doughs can also be deep-fried successfully without a coating or batter to produce sweet and savoury snacks such as donuts, choux pastry aigrettes and Spanish churros. The dough is first shaped by cutting, spooning or piping, then dropped into the oil and cooked until golden. These deep-fried snacks may then be tossed in a sweet or savoury coating, such as sugar or salt.

ROOT VEGETABLE CRISPS

These pretty, colourful crisps (US chips) are perfect to serve with drinks.

1 Peel and trim 1 parsnip, 1 raw beetroot (beet), 1 carrot and 1 potato. Using a mandolin or swivel-bladed vegetable peeler, slice the vegetables into thin shavings.

2 Rinse the vegetable shavings under cold running water to remove any excess starch, then thoroughly pat them dry with kitchen paper, making sure that all the moisture is removed. Spread them out on a layer of kitchen paper until ready to cook.

3 Pour sunflower or vegetable oil into a deep-fat fryer, wok or pan and heat to 180-190°C|350-375°F. Deep-fry the vegetable strips in batches for about 1 minute, or until crisp and golden.

4 Using a draining spoon or wire skimmer, carefully remove the crisps from the hot oil as soon as each batch is cooked and drain on a wire rack lined with a double layer of kitchen paper. Sprinkle the crisps liberally with sea salt and serve immediately.

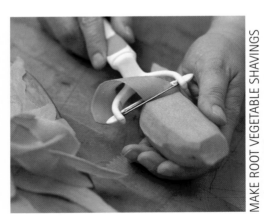
MAKE ROOT VEGETABLE SHAVINGS

HEAT THE OIL

THEN DEEP-FRY UNTIL CRISP

AROMATIC SPICED NUTS

These spicy nuts make a great snack and can be stored in an airtight container for up to a week.

1 Combine 2.5ml | ½ tsp ground star anise, 2.5ml | ½ tsp ground cinnamon, 2.5ml | ½ tsp ground coriander, 2.5ml | ½ tsp ground Sichuan peppercorns, a pinch of ground cloves, 2.5ml | ½ tsp chilli powder and set aside.

2 Bring a large pan of water to a rolling boil and blanch 500g | 1¼lb | 5 cups pecan and walnut halves for 1 minute then drain. (Do not rinse.)

3 Toss the nuts with 115g | 4oz | generous ½ cup golden caster (superfine) sugar in the colander, until the sugar forms a thin glazed coating on the nuts.

4 Deep-fry the nuts in 2-3 batches for 2-3 minutes, then remove with a wire mesh skimmer and transfer to a non-stick baking sheet in a single layer. When cool, transfer to kitchen paper to remove any excess oil.

5 Place the nuts in a bowl and sprinkle the spice mixture over them. Toss to coat well, then season with sea salt.

SPICED DEEP-FRIED NUTS ARE THE PERFECT SNACK TO SERVE WITH DRINKS

SPICED PLANTAIN CHIPS

The slightly sweet flavour of plantain is perfectly offset by the heat of chilli. These are delicious served piping hot with a small bowl of salsa or spicy chilli sauce for dipping.

1 Peel 2 plantains and cut off and discard the ends. Slice the flesh on the diagonal to give larger, flatter pieces, about 1cm/½in thick.

2 Deep-fry the plantain in small batches for about 2 minutes, or until golden.

3 Using a wire skimmer, remove the plantain from the oil and drain on a wire rack lined with kitchen paper.

4 Combine 2.5ml | ½ tsp chilli powder and 5ml | 1 tsp ground cinnamon, sprinkle over the plantain chips and serve immediately.

BITESIZE DEEP-FRIES

These crisp and golden morsels are perfect
for entertaining. Serve with drinks, enjoy
as informal appetizers, or simply snack.
Guests will love the piping hot vegetable
fritters, richly flavoured meatballs, delicate
shellfish and wonderful sauces and dips.

spiky onion and chickpea flour fritters with yogurt and mint chutney

ingredients | SERVES 6-8

225g|8oz|2 cups chickpea (gram) flour

15ml|1 tbsp rice flour

10ml|2 tsp mild or hot chilli powder, according to taste

5ml|1 tsp coarsely ground or crushed coriander seeds

5ml|1 tsp cumin seeds

1.5ml|¼ tsp ground turmeric

5ml|1 tsp sea salt

200ml|7fl oz|scant 1 cup water

2 large onions, halved, thinly sliced and separated into layers

groundnut (peanut) or sunflower oil, for deep-frying

FOR THE CHUTNEY

250ml|8fl oz|1 cup Greek (US strained plain) yogurt

60ml|4 tbsp chopped fresh mint leaves

30ml|2 tbsp mint jelly

1.5ml|¼ tsp finely grated fresh root ginger

1 fresh red chilli, seeded and finely chopped

salt

These fritters are terrific served hot as an appetizer, but they also make a wonderful light snack or lunch when stuffed into a hot crusty roll with a spoonful of yogurt and mint chutney.

1 Combine the chutney ingredients together in a bowl. Season and mix well. Chill until ready to serve.

2 Sift both flours into a large bowl and add the spices and salt. Pour in most of the water and stir to make a thick, pourable batter, adding a little more water if necessary.

3 Add the sliced onions to the batter and mix until thoroughly coated.

4 Heat the oil in a deep-fat fryer or wok to 180°C|350°F. Working in batches, carefully lower spoonfuls of the onion mixture into the hot oil and fry for 3–4 minutes until golden.

5 Remove with a slotted spoon and drain on a wire rack placed over crumpled kitchen paper. Repeat with the rest of the mixture, keeping each batch warm in the oven. Serve immediately, with the chutney.

courgette and parmesan fritters with garlic and mint

These very easy-to-prepare fritters are always popular. They can be enjoyed warm or at room temperature, and are delicious served as a snack to accompany an aperitif or as part of a main course.

ingredients | SERVES 4

750g|1lb 10oz courgettes (zucchini)

40g|1¹/₂oz|¹/₃ cup plain (all-purpose) flour

3 eggs, lightly beaten

1 garlic clove, crushed

45ml|3 tbsp finely grated Parmesan cheese

grated nutmeg

30ml|2 tbsp finely chopped fresh mint leaves

mild olive oil, for frying

salt and ground black pepper

1 Trim and coarsely grate the courgettes by hand or in a food processor fitted with a grating attachment. Place in a large sieve. Press down firmly with the back of a spoon to remove any excess moisture.

2 Place the drained courgettes in a large bowl with the flour, beaten eggs, garlic, grated Parmesan, a pinch of nutmeg and the chopped mint and mix thoroughly. Season well.

3 Pour the olive oil into a large wok or heavy frying pan to a depth of 2cm|³/₄in. Heat to 180°C|350°F.

4 Working in batches, deep-fry spoonfuls of the courgette mixture for 3–4 minutes, turning once, until crisp and golden. Remove with a slotted spoon and drain on a rack lined with kitchen paper. Serve immediately or leave to cool slightly and serve warm or at room temperature.

COOK'S TIP These fritters are delicious served on their own but are also good with a simple, tangy dip. In a bowl, mix together 150ml|¹/₄ pint|²/₃ cup tomato ketchup with 115g|4oz crème fraîche until well blended and serve with the fritters.

italian-style meatballs with a red wine salsa

ingredients | SERVES 4–6

¹/₂ small red onion, finely chopped

500g|1¹/₄lb|5 cups pine nuts, toasted

3 garlic cloves, crushed

60ml|4 tbsp chopped fresh flat leaf parsley

5ml|1 tsp chopped fresh rosemary

10ml|2 tsp fennel seeds, crushed

500g|1¹/₄lb minced (ground) beef

50g|2oz|1 cup fresh breadcrumbs

50g|2oz|¹/₄ cup ricotta cheese

50g|2oz|²/₃ cup finely grated
Parmesan cheese

finely grated rind of 1 large lemon

1 egg

olive oil, for deep-frying

salt and ground black pepper

FOR THE RED WINE SALSA

400g|14oz can chopped tomatoes

15ml|1 tbsp chopped fresh basil leaves

10ml|2 tsp soft light brown sugar

50ml|2fl oz|¹/₄ cup red wine or Marsala

1 Place all the ingredients for the meatballs in a large glass or ceramic bowl and mix well, using your fingers. Season with salt and ground black pepper. Cover the bowl with clear film (plastic wrap) and leave the mixture to rest in the refrigerator overnight for the flavours to mingle and develop.

2 To make the salsa, place all the ingredients in a small pan, season and bring to the boil. Lower the heat and simmer gently for 10 minutes, or until thick and glossy. Set aside.

3 Take golf-ball-size portions of the meatball mixture and roll into balls. Flatten them slightly into a patty shape (about 5cm|2in in diameter) and place on a baking sheet lined with baking parchment.

4 Pour the olive oil into a large, non-stick frying pan or wok to a depth of about 5cm|2in. Heat the oil to about 180°C|350°F. Carefully lower the meatballs into the oil, in batches, and fry for 2–3 minutes, or until cooked through and well browned.

5 Remove with a slotted spoon and drain on a wire rack placed over crumpled kitchen paper. Serve immediately with the red wine salsa.

VARIATIONS These little meatballs are just as good made with minced (ground) chicken, lamb or pork. They can also be made into a delicious sandwich – simply stuffed between slices of toasted ciabatta.

These delicious bitesize meatballs are best made a day in advance, before frying, to allow all the wonderful Italian flavours to blend together. Served with the robust red wine salsa, they make a terrific cocktail party snack.

coconut-rolled prawns
with spicy peanut sauce

These tasty morsels, inspired by the classic Indonesian satay, are great as an hors d'oeuvre with drinks. They also make a great appetizer served warm on a bed of mixed salad leaves.

ingredients | SERVES 6-8

115g|4oz|1 cup plain (all-purpose) flour

5ml|1 tsp baking powder

5ml|1 tsp mild curry powder

2.5ml|½ tsp paprika

5ml|1 tsp sea salt

275ml|9fl oz|generous 1 cup beer

2 large (US extra large) eggs, lightly beaten

200g|7oz|3½ cups desiccated (dry unsweetened shredded) coconut

24 raw tiger prawns (jumbo shrimp), peeled and tails intact

sunflower oil, for deep-frying

FOR THE DIPPING SAUCE

15ml|1 tbsp smooth peanut butter

15ml|1 tbsp dark soy sauce

45ml|3 tbsp sweet chilli sauce

45ml|3 tbsp crème fraîche

1 garlic clove, finely minced (ground) or crushed

finely grated rind of 1 lime

juice of 2 large limes

1 To make the dipping sauce, place all the sauce ingredients in a bowl and mix well until combined. Cover the bowl with clear film (plastic wrap) and place in the refrigerator or in a cool place until required.

2 In a large mixing bowl, combine the flour, baking powder, curry powder, paprika and sea salt. Add the beer and the lightly beaten eggs, and stir until just combined. (Take care not to overmix as this will spoil the batter.) Gently fold in 25g|1oz|½ cup of the desiccated coconut.

3 Carefully thread each prawn lengthways, from head to tail, on to the tip of a bamboo skewer.

4 Spread the remaining desiccated coconut in a deep soup plate or a wide, shallow bowl.

5 Pour the sunflower oil into a deep wok to a depth of 7.5cm|3in and heat to 190°C|375°F.

6 Working in two to three batches, dip the skewered prawns into the batter (letting the excess batter drip back into the bowl), then lightly coat them all over in the coconut.

7 Deep-fry, in batches, for about 3 minutes, or until lightly golden. Drain on a wire rack placed over crumpled kitchen paper and serve immediately with the dipping sauce.

tempura with ginger dipping sauce

ingredients | SERVES 4

50g|2oz|1/2 cup rice flour

100g|3³/₄oz|scant 1 cup plain (all-purpose) flour

2.5ml|1/2 tsp baking powder

2 large (US extra large) egg whites, lightly beaten

350–400ml|12–14fl oz|1¹/₂–1²/₃ cup ice-cold soda water (club soda)

sunflower oil, for deep-frying

8 raw tiger prawns (jumbo shrimp), peeled, with tails intact

300g|11oz assorted vegetables, such as sliced sweet potato, broccoli florets, baby spinach leaves, courgette (zucchini) slices, enokitake mushrooms, sliced red and yellow (bell) pepper

FOR THE DIPPING SAUCE

5cm|2in piece of fresh root ginger, peeled and cut into thin slivers

100ml|6¹/₂ tbsp soy sauce

50ml|3¹/₂ tbsp sweet sherry

50ml|3¹/₂ tbsp rice vinegar

15ml|1 tbsp soft light brown sugar

This delectable Japanese dish of vegetables and prawns coated in a light-as-air batter, and served with a ginger-infused soy sauce, must be served as soon as it is cooked to gain maximum satisfaction.

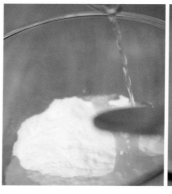

1 First make the sauce. Place all the ingredients in a small pan and bring to the boil. Lower the heat and cook gently for 1–2 minutes. Remove from the heat and leave to cool. Cover and set aside at room temperature for 1–2 hours to let the flavours develop.

2 Preheat the oven to low. For the tempura, mix the flours, baking powder, beaten egg whites and soda water and stir until just combined. (Do not overmix or the batter will become heavy. The mixture should be lumpy.)

3 Pour the oil into a deep-fat fryer or a wok to a depth of 7.5cm|3in and heat to 180°C|350°F.

4 Working in batches, dip the prawns and vegetables in the batter, shaking off the excess batter, and deep-fry for 2–3 minutes, or until golden. Drain the cooked tempura on a wire rack lined with kitchen paper, then transfer to another wire rack (with no paper) and place in the oven to keep warm. Cook the remaining tempura and serve immediately with the dipping sauce.

CRISP AND APPETIZING

These delicious deep-fries are a great
way to start a meal. Inspired by classic
recipes from around the world, there is a
wonderful selection of both simple and
sophisticated dishes that are perfect for
relaxed and formal dining alike.

potato röstis with smoked salmon

ingredients | MAKES 12–15

500g|1¼lb floury potatoes

2 spring onions (scallions), thinly sliced

1 large (US extra large) egg

30ml|2 tbsp plain (all-purpose) flour

sunflower oil, for frying

250g|9oz smoked salmon

150ml|¼ pint|⅔ cup crème fraîche

salt and ground black pepper

chopped fresh dill or chives and caviar or salmon roe, to garnish

VARIATION To make röstis with a slightly different flavour, replace the potatoes with a mixture of 250g| 9oz potatoes and 250g|9oz celeriac or swede (rutabaga).

1 Preheat the oven to low. Peel and grate the potatoes and place with the spring onions in a sieve. Press down with the back of a spoon to squeeze out as much starch as possible. Transfer to a bowl and add the egg and flour. Season and mix well.

2 Pour the oil into a large, deep non-stick frying pan or wok to a depth of 2cm|¾in and heat until it reaches 180°C|350°F or when a cube of bread browns in 45–60 seconds.

3 Carefully place a tablespoon of the potato mixture in the oil, flattening it slightly with the back of a spoon to form a small pancake about 5cm|2in in diameter.

4 Keep adding more tablespoonfuls of the mixture, cooking in small batches, and fry for 1 minute until golden on the underside. Flip over and cook for 1–2 minutes more until golden.

5 Remove the röstis from the pan with a skimmer or slotted spoon and drain on a wire rack lined with kitchen paper. Transfer the röstis to a baking sheet and keep warm in the oven while you cook the remaining mixture.

6 Cut the salmon into thin strips. Place the röstis on a serving plate and top each one with a spoonful of crème fraîche and strips of smoked salmon. Garnish with dill or chives and a little caviar or salmon roe.

The humble potato is transformed into an impressive and sophisticated appetizer when it is flavoured with spring onion and fried into little crisp golden pancakes, then topped with crème fraîche and strips of smoked salmon.

stuffed mozzarella and risotto balls with quick pesto dip

These golden risotto croquettes filled with melting mozzarella are an excellent way of using up leftover risotto. The glutinous texture of the rice keeps the grains together.

ingredients | MAKES 24

45ml | 3 tbsp unsalted (sweet) butter

4 spring onions (scallions), thinly sliced

400g | 14oz | 2 cups risotto rice

1.5 litres | 2½ pints | 6¼ cups good quality chicken stock, simmering

100g | 3¾oz | scant 1 cup finely grated Pecorino cheese

45ml | 3 tbsp finely chopped parsley

2 eggs, lightly beaten

200g | 7oz mozzarella cheese, cut into 24 cubes (about 1cm | ½in square)

200g | 7oz | 1¾ cups dried breadcrumbs

sunflower oil, for deep-frying

salt and ground black pepper

FOR THE DIP

45ml | 3 tbsp good quality fresh green pesto

30ml | 2 tbsp mayonnaise

15ml | 1 tbsp crème fraîche

1 Make the dip. In a bowl, combine the pesto, mayonnaise and crème fraîche, then cover and set aside.

2 Melt the butter in a large pan over a medium-low heat. Add the spring onions and cook for 2–3 minutes until just softened.

3 Add the rice to the pan and cook for 1–2 minutes to seal. Add two ladlefuls of the hot stock, stirring constantly. Keep adding ladlefuls of the stock to just cover the rice, and continue cooking in this way for 20 minutes, or until the rice is *al dente*.

4 Remove from the heat and stir in the Pecorino, parsley and eggs. Season well and spread the risotto on a large baking sheet to cool completely.

5 When the rice is cool, divide the mixture into 24 portions. Take one portion in the palm of your hand and place a cube of mozzarella in the centre. Fold the rice over to encase the cheese and press the mixture into a neat ball. Repeat with the remaining portions of rice mixture and cubes of mozzarella cheese.

6 Place the breadcrumbs on a large plate and roll each ball to coat evenly.

7 Pour the oil into a deep-fat fryer or a wok to a depth of 6cm | 2½in and heat to 180°C | 350°F. Add the risotto balls, in batches, and deep-fry for 3–4 minutes, or until golden brown. Drain on a wire rack placed over crumpled kitchen paper. Serve hot with the pesto dip.

lamb samosas with coconut and coriander relish

ingredients | MAKES 24

30ml|2 tbsp sunflower oil

1 medium potato, peeled and finely chopped

1 small onion, finely chopped

1 garlic clove, crushed

15ml|1 tbsp medium or hot curry paste

200g|7oz minced (ground) lamb

50g|2oz|1/2 cup peas, thawed if frozen

30ml|2 tbsp chopped fresh mint

30ml|2 tbsp chopped fresh
coriander (cilantro)

vegetable oil, for deep-frying

FOR THE RELISH

100g|3³/₄oz freshly grated coconut flesh

1 green chilli, seeded and finely chopped

5ml|1 tsp finely grated fresh root ginger

60ml|4 tbsp thick natural (plain) yogurt

120ml|8 tbsp chopped fresh
coriander (cilantro)

salt

FOR THE PASTRY

400g|14oz|3¹/₂ cups plain
(all-purpose) flour

5ml|1 tsp salt

5ml|1 tsp roasted cumin seeds

75–90ml|5–6 tbsp vegetable
or sunflower oil

Originally a popular street snack from northern India, these stuffed pastries are delicious served warm with the cool, aromatic relish. They can be made in advance and warmed in a medium-hot oven.

1 Combine the relish ingredients in a bowl. Season, cover and chill.

2 To make the filling, heat the oil in a frying pan and stir-fry the potato, onion and garlic for 5 minutes. Add the curry paste and cook, stirring, for 1 minute, then add the lamb. Stir-fry for 5 minutes until sealed, then add 30ml|2 tbsp water, lower the heat, cover and simmer for 20 minutes.

3 Add the peas and herbs to the lamb, season and cook for 3–4 minutes. Remove from the heat and set aside.

4 Make the pastry. Mix the plain flour, salt and cumin seeds in a bowl. Add the oil and 200ml|7fl oz|scant 1 cup water to make a soft dough. Turn out on to a lightly floured surface and knead for 5–6 minutes. Divide into 12 portions and roll out each piece to a 13–15cm| 5–6in round, then cut in half.

5 Fold each pastry semicircle into a cone shape. Place a spoonful of the filling in each semicircle. Dampen the edges with water and press the edges to seal completely. Repeat with the remaining pastry.

6 Heat the oil in a deep-fat fryer or wok to 180°C|350°F and deep-fry the samosas, in batches, for 3–4 minutes, until pale golden and crisp. Lift out with a skimmer and drain on a wire rack placed over crumpled kitchen paper. Serve with the relish.

crisp and crunchy pork, prawn and vegetable spring rolls

Minced pork and prawns combined with crunchy stir-fried vegetables and delicately flavoured soy sauce and sesame oil are brought to life with the robust flavours of ginger and garlic.

ingredients | MAKES 20

250g|9oz minced (ground) pork

200g|7oz raw peeled prawns (shrimp), chopped

75ml|5 tbsp light soy sauce

10ml|2 tsp sesame oil

50ml|2fl oz|1/4 cup Chinese rice wine

7.5ml|11/2 tsp cornflour (cornstarch)

6 dried Chinese mushrooms

2.5ml|1/2 tsp ground black pepper

60ml|4 tbsp vegetable oil

15ml|1 tbsp finely grated fresh root ginger

3 garlic cloves, crushed

100g|33/4oz Chinese leaves (Chinese cabbage), finely shredded

150g|5oz carrots, peeled and finely shredded

30ml|2 tbsp finely chopped fresh chives

150g|5oz|2/3 cup beansprouts

1 egg yolk

30ml|2 tbsp plain (all-purpose) flour

20 spring roll wrappers

vegetable oil, for deep-frying

sweet chilli sauce, to serve

1 Place the pork and prawns in a large bowl. Mix 30ml|2 tbsp of the soy sauce, 5ml|1 tsp of the sesame oil, 25ml|11/2 tbsp of the rice wine and 5ml|1 tsp of the cornflour. Add to the pork and toss well. Cover and leave to marinate in the refrigerator for 1 hour.

2 Soak the mushrooms in hot water for 30 minutes, drain and squeeze out any excess moisture. Shred the caps.

3 Combine the remaining soy sauce, sesame oil and cornflour with the black pepper in a bowl and set aside.

4 Heat 30ml|2 tbsp of the vegetable oil in a wok. Stir-fry the pork mixture for 3–4 minutes until sealed. Remove from the wok and set aside. Wipe out the wok, reheat over a high heat and add the remaining oil.

5 Stir-fry the mushrooms, ginger and garlic for 20 seconds, then add the Chinese leaves, carrots, the remaining wine, the chives, beansprouts and soy mixture. Stir-fry for 1 minute. Return the pork mixture to the wok and cook for 2–3 minutes until thickened. Drain in a colander and leave to cool.

6 Mix the egg yolk, flour and 45ml| 3 tbsp water. Place 30ml|2 tbsp of the pork filling on the corner of each wrapper. Brush some egg yolk mixture on the opposite corner. Fold in the remaining corners and roll up into a cylinder, pressing the edges to secure.

7 Heat 7.5cm|3in oil in a wok to 190°C|375°F. Deep-fry the spring rolls, in batches, for 5 minutes, turning once, or until golden and crisp. Drain and serve with the chilli sauce.

crispy rice noodle and asparagus salad

ingredients | SERVES 4

24 asparagus spears, trimmed

1 red (bell) pepper, seeded and thinly sliced

15ml|1 tbsp sunflower or light olive oil

2.5ml|$\frac{1}{2}$ tsp sesame oil

90ml|6 tbsp light soy sauce

10ml|2 tsp clear honey

45ml|3 tbsp sherry

1 garlic clove, finely minced (ground)

1.5ml|$\frac{1}{4}$ tsp finely grated fresh root ginger

30ml|2 tbsp toasted sesame seeds

salt and ground black pepper

FOR THE NOODLES

sunflower oil, for deep-frying

50–65g|2–2$\frac{1}{2}$oz thin rice noodles

This salad is a delicious fusion of colours and textures. Lightly cooked asparagus and red pepper are combined with a piquant Asian-style dressing and topped with crispy rice noodles to make a perfect appetizer for elegant dining.

1 Heat a large pan of lightly salted water until boiling. Add the asparagus and bring the water back to the boil. Cook the asparagus for 3–4 minutes, or until just tender. Drain and refresh under cold water, then drain again. Place the spears in a large, shallow dish with the red pepper.

2 Mix together the sunflower or light olive oil, sesame oil, light soy sauce, honey, sherry, garlic and ginger in a jug (pitcher). Season well.

3 Pour the dressing over the asparagus and peppers. Toss to combine, then sprinkle the sesame seeds over the top of the salad.

4 Pour the oil for deep-frying into a large wok to a depth of 4–5cm| 1$\frac{1}{2}$–2in and heat to 180°C|350°F.

5 Divide the rice noodles into four portions and deep-fry each one separately. They will puff up as soon as they hit the hot oil. Immediately remove them with a skimmer or a slotted spoon and drain on a wire rack lined with kitchen paper.

6 To serve the salad, divide the asparagus and peppers among four large plates. Top the salad with the crispy noodles. Drizzle over any remaining dressing and serve immediately.

THE BIG FRY

Battered fish, piping hot crab cakes,
crisply coated meat and poultry and deep-
fried vegetables can all make fabulous
main meals. This chapter is devoted to
hearty dishes with rich, satisfying flavours
and delicious accompaniments.

veal parmigiano with garlic mashed potatoes and salsa fresca

ingredients | SERVES 4

4 x 175g|6oz boneless veal cutlets (rib chops)

75g|3oz|1 cup finely grated Parmesan cheese

3 large (US extra large) eggs

15ml|1 tbsp finely chopped fresh rosemary leaves

600g|1lb 5oz|generous 8½ cups dried breadcrumbs

olive oil, for deep-frying

salt and ground black pepper

FOR THE MASHED POTATOES

675g|1½lb floury potatoes, peeled and coarsely chopped

25g|1oz|2 tbsp butter

150ml|¼ pint|⅔ cup crème fraîche

1 garlic clove, finely crushed

60ml|4 tbsp chopped fresh flat leaf parsley

FOR THE SALSA

4 ripe plum tomatoes, chopped

small handful basil leaves, coarsely torn

30ml|2 tbsp extra virgin olive oil

15ml|1 tbsp balsamic vinegar

1 Make the mashed potatoes. Boil the potatoes in a large pan of lightly salted water for 12 minutes, or until tender, then drain and return to the pan. Add the butter, crème fraîche and garlic to the potatoes and mash until smooth. Add the parsley, season and stir to mix well. Cover and keep warm.

2 Place all the salsa ingredients in a bowl, season and stir until well combined. Cover and set aside.

3 Pat the veal cutlets dry with kitchen paper. Place the cheese in a shallow dish. Lightly beat the eggs with the rosemary and seasoning in another dish. Place the breadcrumbs in a third shallow bowl or on a plate.

4 Line a baking sheet with baking parchment. Dip each cutlet into the cheese to coat evenly, then into the egg and, finally, into the breadcrumbs. Set aside on the baking sheet.

5 Pour the olive oil into a large, heavy pan to a depth of 2.5cm|1in and heat until very hot but not smoking. Carefully add the cutlets to the hot oil and fry for 7–8 minutes, turning once, until lightly golden. Transfer with a slotted spoon to a wire rack placed over crumpled kitchen paper to drain.

6 To serve, divide the mashed potatoes among four warmed plates and top each with a veal cutlet. Serve the salsa on the side.

Succulent cutlets of veal, delicately flavoured with rosemary and Parmesan cheese, are protected by a delightful crisp coating. They are served with luxurious mashed potatoes flavoured with parsley and garlic and accompanied by a fresh tomato and basil salsa.

fish and chips with fusion tartare sauce

ingredients | SERVES 4

4 x 200–250g|7–9oz thick cod, haddock or halibut fillets

FOR THE BATTER

100g|3¾oz|scant 1 cup plain (all-purpose) flour

20g|¾oz|3 tbsp rice flour

5ml|1 tsp salt

10ml|2 tsp cayenne pepper

175ml|6fl oz|¾ cup beer

FOR THE CHIPS (FRENCH FRIES)

900g|2lb floury potatoes, peeled and cut into 2cm|¾in sticks, kept in iced water until ready to cook

sunflower oil, for deep-frying

FOR THE SAUCE

150ml|¼ pint|⅔ cup good quality mayonnaise

finely grated rind and juice of 1 lime

15ml|1 tbsp capers

30ml|2 tbsp chopped gherkins

1 fresh red chilli, seeded and finely chopped

1 spring onion (scallion), thinly sliced

30ml|2 tbsp finely chopped fresh coriander (cilantro) leaves

Juicy fillets of fish are coated in a spiced beer batter that becomes wonderfully crisp and crunchy when cooked. They are delicious served with double-fried chips and tartare sauce with a twist.

1 Combine the sauce ingredients in a bowl, then cover and set aside.

2 Whisk together all the batter ingredients in a bowl. Cover and leave to stand in the refrigerator.

3 Preheat the oven to low. Pour the oil into a deep-fat fryer or a large, heavy pan, with a fitted basket, to a depth of 16–17cm|6¼–6½in. Heat to 160°C|325°F.

4 Drain the potato sticks and pat thoroughly dry on kitchen paper. Deep-fry the chips, in four to five batches, for 5-6 minutes. Drain.

5 Increase the temperature of the oil to 190°C|375°F. Cook the chips, in batches, for 3–4 minutes, until golden and crisp. Drain well on kitchen paper, transfer to a wire rack set on a baking sheet and keep warm in the oven.

6 Pat the fish dry with kitchen paper and dip two fish fillets into the batter to coat evenly. Carefully lower into the oil (still at 190°C|375°F). Deep-fry for 4–5 minutes, or until golden and cooked through. Drain on a wire rack placed over crumpled kitchen paper, then transfer to a wire rack or baking sheet and keep warm in the oven. Repeat with the remaining fillets.

7 To serve, place the fish on four warmed serving plates with the chips and tartare sauce.

crab cakes with coconut rice

ingredients | SERVES 4

2 eggs, lightly beaten

100g|3³/₄oz|scant 1 cup plain
(all-purpose) flour

vegetable oil, for deep-frying

FOR THE CRAB CAKES

250g|9oz|4¹/₂ cups fresh white breadcrumbs

500g|1¹/₄lb fresh white crab meat

4 spring onions (scallions), finely chopped

1 fresh red chilli, seeded and finely chopped

90ml|6 tbsp chopped fresh coriander
(cilantro) leaves

1 garlic clove, crushed

90ml|6 tbsp good quality mayonnaise

5ml|1 tsp finely grated lime rind

salt and ground black pepper

FOR THE RICE

30ml|2 tbsp sunflower oil

10ml|2 tsp brown mustard seeds

10ml|2 tsp cumin seeds

1 dried red chilli

225g|8oz|generous 1 cup basmati rice,
rinsed and soaked for 30 minutes, drained

105ml|7 tbsp coconut milk

375ml|13fl oz|generous 1¹/₂ cups hot water

chopped fresh coriander (cilantro) and
chives, to garnish

These terrific crab cakes can be made and cooked hours in advance and then reheated in a low oven while the rice is cooking, thus making a very impressive, no-hassle main meal.

1 Combine all the ingredients for the crab cakes in a large bowl. Season and chill for at least 1 hour.

2 Meanwhile, prepare the rice. Heat the oil in a non-stick pan. Add the mustard and cumin seeds and dried red chilli. When the seeds start to pop, add the rice and gently stir-fry for 1–2 minutes. Add the coconut milk and hot water, season and bring to the boil. Cover tightly, reduce the heat and cook for 15 minutes. Remove from the heat and set aside, still covered, for a further 15 minutes.

3 Divide the crab mixture into 12 portions and form them into cakes. Place the eggs in a shallow bowl and the flour on a plate. Dip each cake into the egg, then into the flour to coat, patting away any excess flour.

4 Pour the oil into a large, deep non-stick pan to a depth of 4–5cm| 1¹/₂–2in, and heat to 180°C|350°F. Deep-fry the cakes, in batches, for 2–3 minutes, turning once, until crisp and golden. Remove with a slotted spoon and drain on a wire rack placed over crumpled kitchen paper.

5 To serve, fluff up the coconut rice with a fork and divide among four warmed plates. Top each with three crab cakes and garnish with chopped coriander and chives.

southern-fried chicken
with caesar-style salad

The flavours of the American southern states are given a tasty new angle with these tender, spicy marinated chicken drumsticks served with crisp salad leaves in a deliciously lemony dressing.

ingredients | SERVES 4

8 large chicken drumsticks

500ml|17fl oz|generous 2 cups buttermilk

15ml|1 tbsp Tabasco or hot red pepper sauce

150g|5oz|1¼ cups plain (all-purpose) flour

sunflower oil, for deep-frying

salt and ground black pepper

FOR THE SALAD

2 Little Gem (Bibb) lettuces

3 heads of red or green chicory (Belgian endive)

5–6 canned anchovies, drained

1 garlic clove, crushed

5ml|1 tsp Dijon mustard

30ml|2 tbsp extra virgin olive oil

5ml|1 tsp finely grated lemon rind

75ml|5 tbsp crème fraîche

juice of ½ lemon

25g|1oz|⅓ cup finely grated Parmesan cheese

1 Rinse the chicken drumsticks and pat dry. Make a couple of deep slashes in each drumstick with a sharp knife and place in a large glass or ceramic bowl. Mix the buttermilk and Tabasco or pepper sauce and pour over the chicken. Toss to coat. Cover and marinate in the refrigerator overnight.

2 Preheat the oven to 180°C|350°F| Gas 4. Place the flour in a plastic bag and season. Drain the chicken and toss in the flour, a few pieces at a time, to coat. Set aside on a baking sheet lined with baking parchment for 20 minutes to set the coating.

3 Pour the oil into a deep-fat fryer or a wok to a depth of 5–6cm|2–2½in and heat to 180°C|350°F.

4 Deep-fry the chicken, in batches, for 10–12 minutes. Transfer to a wire rack placed on a baking sheet and put in the oven for 15 minutes, or until the chicken is cooked through.

5 Meanwhile, separate the salad leaves, rinse and pat or spin dry. Place in a large bowl. Crush the anchovies to a paste in a mortar using a pestle. Add the garlic and mustard and gradually beat in the olive oil and lemon rind. Season and stir in the crème fraîche and lemon juice.

6 Toss the leaves with the dressing and heap on to four serving plates, then scatter the cheese on top. Place two drumsticks on each plate and serve immediately.

warm aubergine and fragrant herb salad with griddled garlic ciabatta

ingredients | SERVES 4

olive oil, for deep-frying

3 aubergines (eggplant), thinly sliced lengthways

small handful coarsely torn fresh mint leaves

small handful coarsely torn fresh basil leaves

small handful fresh flat leaf parsley

2 plum or vine tomatoes, peeled, seeded and finely diced

30ml|2 tbsp toasted pine nuts

pomegranate seeds, to garnish (optional)

FOR THE DRESSING

75ml|5 tbsp extra virgin olive oil

juice of 2 lemons

1 fresh red chilli, seeded and finely chopped

5ml|1 tsp soft light brown sugar

1 garlic clove, crushed

salt and ground black pepper

FOR THE CIABATTA

8 long slices ciabatta

4 garlic cloves, peeled and halved

Fried slices of aubergine mixed with fragrant herbs and tossed in a piquant dressing with tomatoes and jewel-like pomegranate seeds make for a sophisticated dish at a stylish dinner or lunch party.

1 Pour the oil into a deep-fat fryer, wok or heavy pan to a depth of 4cm|1½in and heat to 180°C|350°F.

2 Preheat the oven to low. Working in batches, fry the aubergine slices for about 2 minutes, or until golden brown, lift out with a wire mesh skimmer or slotted spoon and drain on crumpled kitchen paper. Transfer to a wire rack or baking sheet and place in the oven to keep warm.

3 Make the dressing. Combine all the ingredients in a bowl or jug (pitcher). Season and set aside.

4 Heat a ridged griddle pan until hot and griddle the ciabatta slices on both sides or toast under a grill (broiler).

5 Gently rub each slice of ciabatta with a garlic half to flavour well. Discard the garlic.

6 To assemble the salad, place the aubergines in a large shallow serving dish with the herbs and tomatoes. Pour the dressing over the top and toss gently to mix. Sprinkle over the pine nuts and the pomegranate seeds, if using, and serve immediately with the garlic ciabatta slices.

SWEET AND SIZZLING

Freshly cooked donuts dusted with sugar
and sumptuous deep-fried desserts are
the ultimate indulgence. This inspired
collection of sweet treats will make the
perfect end to any meal and satisfy
even the sweetest tooth.

american-style sugared donuts

ingredients | MAKES ABOUT 12–15

60g|2¹/₄oz|generous 4 tbsp unsalted (sweet) butter

60g|2¹/₄oz|generous ¹/₄ cup caster (superfine) sugar

1 large (US extra large) egg, beaten

90ml|6 tbsp buttermilk

225g|8oz|2 cups plain (all-purpose) flour

5ml|1 tsp baking powder

2.5ml|¹/₂ tsp bicarbonate of soda (baking soda)

pinch of salt

finely grated rind of 1 orange

5ml|1 tsp ground cinnamon

pinch of grated nutmeg

vegetable oil, for deep-frying

icing (confectioners') sugar, for dusting

These irresistible, all-time favourite donuts are cooked without yeast for a shorter preparation time and almost instant results. They are perfect with a mug of hot chocolate or strong milky coffee.

1 Place the butter, sugar, beaten egg and buttermilk in a large bowl. Sift over the flour, baking powder, bicarbonate of soda and salt. Add the orange rind, cinnamon and nutmeg and mix using a wooden spoon until well-mixed and smooth.

2 Turn the mixture out on to a lightly floured work surface. With floured hands, knead the dough for about 5 minutes until it becomes really smooth and slightly soft and elastic but not sticky.

3 Roll out the dough on a lightly floured surface to about 1.5cm/²/₃in thick and stamp out rounds using a 5cm|2in cutter.

4 Press a hole in the centre of each dough round with the handle of a wooden spoon to make a ring shape.

5 Pour the oil into a deep-fat fryer, wok or large, heavy pan and heat to 180°C|350°F.

6 Fry the donuts, in batches, for about 5 minutes, or until browned and cooked through. Lift out with a skimmer and drain on a wire rack lined with kitchen paper.

7 Leave the donuts to cool slightly, then dust with sifted icing sugar and serve warm.

cinnamon and apple fritters

ingredients | SERVES 4-6

3–4 tart eating apples such as Granny Smith, peeled, cored and sliced into 1cm|½in rings

50ml|2fl oz|¼ cup Marsala

3 eggs, beaten

125g|4¼oz|generous 1 cup plain (all-purpose) flour

30g|1¼oz|generous 2 tbsp golden caster (superfine) sugar

5ml|1 tsp ground cinnamon

2.5ml|½ tsp salt

vegetable oil, for deep-frying

berries, to decorate

caster (superfine) sugar, for dusting

crème fraîche or whipped double (heavy) cream, to serve

1 Place the apple slices in a large, shallow bowl and pour over the Marsala, turning to coat them evenly. Cover and set aside to macerate for about 1 hour.

2 Beat together the eggs, flour, sugar, cinnamon and salt in a large bowl until thick and smooth. Drain the apples and set aside, reserving the Marsala. Add enough of the Marsala to the batter to make a coating consistency. Beat until smooth and free of lumps.

3 Add the apples to the batter and stir gently to coat evenly. Heat the oil in a deep-fat fryer or a large, heavy pan to 180°C|350°F.

4 Working in three or four batches, gently lower the apple rings into the oil, and deep-fry for 3–4 minutes until golden. Remove with a slotted spoon and drain on a wire rack placed over crumpled kitchen paper.

5 Divide the fritters among warmed serving plates and decorate with berries. Dust with caster sugar and serve immediately with crème fraîche or whipped cream.

VARIATIONS Chunky slices or wedges of pear or tiny bananas are also good dipped in this batter and deep-fried. Choose bananas that are not too ripe or a well-flavoured variety of pear with a firm flesh.

Served piping hot, these slices of crisp apple in a fluffy, cinnamon-scented, light-as-air batter, will fill the house with an irresistible aroma. They are popular with children and adults alike.

crisp mango stacks with raspberry and passion fruit coulis

ingredients | SERVES 4

vegetable oil, for deep-frying

12 wonton wrappers

icing (confectioners') sugar, for dusting

FOR THE FILLING

2 ripe mangoes, peeled, stoned (pitted) and finely diced

1 piece of preserved stem ginger in syrup, drained

5ml|1 tsp ginger syrup from the jar

FOR THE RASPBERRY COULIS

250g|9oz|1½ cups raspberries

25g|1oz|¼ cup icing (confectioners') sugar

FOR THE PASSION FRUIT COULIS

4 passion fruits

15ml|1 tbsp caster (superfine) sugar

This luscious dessert is very easy to prepare. The wonderful colours and flavours of mango, ginger, raspberries and passion fruit, coupled with crisp wonton sheets, will leave you longing for more.

1 First make the raspberry coulis by pressing the raspberries through a fine metal sieve. Discard the seeds and mix the sieved purée with the icing sugar. Chill until needed.

2 Then make the passion fruit coulis. Remove the seeds and pulp from the fruit and place in a small pan with the sugar. Heat gently until the sugar dissolves, then remove from the heat and set aside. Chill until needed.

3 To make the filling, place the diced mangoes in a bowl. Finely chop the preserved ginger, add to the mangoes with the ginger syrup and mix well.

4 Pour the oil in a deep-fryer or wok to a depth of 2cm|¾in and heat to 180°C|350°F. Deep-fry the wonton wrappers, one at a time, sandwiching each wrapper between two slotted spatulas to help them stay flat. Cook for 2–3 minutes, or until crisp and golden, then drain on a wire rack placed over crumpled kitchen paper.

5 To serve, place a wonton wrapper on each of four plates and top with a spoonful of mango mixture. Add another wrapper and a spoonful of mango mixture, then top with a third wrapper. Dust with sugar and drizzle the coulis around. Serve immediately.

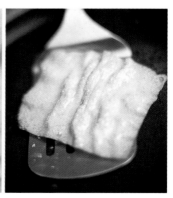

nutty banana wontons
with caramel chocolate sauce

These delightful little parcels are filled with a nutty banana mixture and served with a decadent caramel chocolate sauce, for a delicious end to a meal.

ingredients | MAKES 24

200g|7oz peeled and mashed bananas

50g|2oz|1/2 cup chopped walnuts

25g|1oz|1/4 cup chopped hazelnuts

50g|2oz|1/2 cup chopped pecan nuts

30ml|2 tbsp sweetened desiccated (dry shredded) coconut

10ml|2 tsp soft light brown sugar

24 wonton wrappers
(about 8cm|3¼in square)

vegetable oil, for deep-frying

icing (confectioners') sugar, for dusting

finely chopped mixed nuts, to decorate

FOR THE SAUCE

2 x 50g|2oz caramel-filled chocolate bars

150ml|1/4 pint|2/3 cup double (heavy) cream

1 Place the mashed banana, walnuts, hazelnuts, pecans, coconut and soft brown sugar in a large bowl and mix to form a thick paste.

2 Lay the wonton wrappers on a lightly floured work surface and, working quickly, place a teaspoonful of the banana and nut mixture in the centre of each one. Dampen the edges of the wrappers with water, gather the sides around the filling and pinch the edges to form a little "purse".

3 Preheat the oven to low. Pour the oil into a deep-fat fryer or wok to a depth of 4–5cm|1½–2in. Heat to 180°C|350°F.

4 Deep-fry the wontons, in batches, for 3–4 minutes, or until golden and crisp. Drain on a wire rack placed over crumpled kitchen paper. Transfer to the oven to keep warm.

5 To make the sauce, cut the chocolate bars into small pieces and place in a small heavy pan with the cream. Heat gently until the chocolate bars have melted and stir until the sauce is smooth.

6 To serve, place the wontons on a warm serving plate and dust lightly with sifted icing sugar. Drizzle with the sauce and sprinkle with finely chopped mixed nuts.

deep-fried cherries in white wine batter

Fresh fruit coated with a simple batter and then deep-fried is a favourite recipe found in some shape or form in all the different cuisines of the world. Apples, bananas, plums and pears can all be used as an alternative to the cherries in this recipe.

ingredients | SERVES 4–6

450g|1lb ripe red cherries, on their stalks

120g|4¹/₄oz|generous 1 cup plain (all-purpose) flour

60g|2¹/₄oz|generous ¹/₄ cup golden caster (superfine) sugar

75ml|5 tbsp full-fat (whole) milk

75ml|5 tbsp dry white wine

3 eggs, beaten

vegetable oil, for deep-frying

icing (confectioners') sugar and ground cinnamon, for dusting

vanilla ice cream, to serve

VARIATION For a really crunchy coating, stir 50g|2oz lightly crushed cornflakes into the batter just before coating the cherries.

1 Gently wash the cherries and pat dry with kitchen paper. Tie the stalks together with fine string to form clusters of four or five cherries.

2 Place the flour, golden caster sugar, milk, white wine and eggs in a mixing bowl and stir thoroughly to make a smooth batter.

3 Pour the vegetable oil into a deep-fat fryer or large, heavy pan and heat to 190°C|375°F.

4 Working in batches, half-dip each cherry cluster into the batter and then carefully drop the cluster into the hot oil. Fry for 3–4 minutes until golden. Remove the deep-fried cherries with a wire-mesh skimmer or slotted spoon and drain on a wire rack placed over crumpled kitchen paper.

5 Lightly dust the deep-fried cherries with icing sugar and cinnamon and serve immediately with scoops of vanilla ice cream.

INDEX